Grace Looks Good On You

WHEN GRACE BECOMES PERSONAL

EXPANDED EDITION

BY DENNIS PAUL GOLDSWORTHY-DAVIS

Open Wells Ministries

15315 Capital Port

San Antonio, TX 78249

www.openwellsministries.org

ACKNOWLEDGEMENTS

I would like to give special thanks to Jeannie Hartman who inspired me to continue to write and has helped me intensely.

Also to my local church, Great Grace International, who have been a great testimony of the grace of God.

DEDICATION

I dedicate this book to my beautiful wife Christine without whom there would never have been such a walk of grace. My personal trophy of grace in action.

Library of Congress Number:

ISBN-13: 978-0-9979192-9-5

Printed in the United States of America by Open Wells Ministries

TABLE OF CONTENTS

FOREWORD

GRACE LOOKS GOOD ON YOU

Dennis Goldsworthy-Davis

Some people have a real gift to teach on subjects that they have searched and studied. Others have the gift of living the message they preach. They become what the Apostle Paul called, "Living Epistles," and such is Dennis Goldsworthy-Davis.

I met Dennis in the late 1980's. My brother was ministering at the church where Dennis was on staff. I hadn't met or known of Dennis and had never even heard his name. At the end of the service, the pastor of the church had asked Dennis to come up and pray and release a "prophetic" word to close out the night. Needless to say, Dennis came up and began to pray over me and released a prophetic word that changed my life. He had no idea of the conversation that my brother and I had on the flight to San Antonio. I was so overwhelmed with it all that I dropped to my knees, so overcome by the power of God and the confirming word from this man whom I have never met.

Dennis and I became lifelong friends. It is with great honor that I write this simple forward for this expanded version of "When Grace Becomes Personal". Dennis not only became my friend, but the most trusted voice in my life as we launched our new church in 1996. He was by far the most frequent guest speaker and friend, that I had come to help me build the people of our church family. Dennis became the main prophetic and confirming voice really in my life.

This foreword isn't just about the book, but about the author. There is not a teaching or a message that Dennis has preached that did not impact my life or the life of those who had ears to hear. He's not only a great teacher but carries one of the most accurate prophetic voices I've ever heard. After all these years, Dennis continues to impact my life and now through his new book, "When Grace Becomes Personal," your life is going to radically change.

If someone gives you the title and keys to his car and turns around and walks away and you never see him again, then you have received a free gift. But if that person says to you, "You have to wash and wax this car if you want me to give it to you", then it was not free, but you had to earn it. This book is Dennis giving you the title and keys to his life message. You can sit and stare at the car and leave it parked in your driveway. Or you can open door, open the pages of this life changing book and go for the ride of your life.

There is no doubt in my mind that this book will help answer a desperate cry around the world, from people who are desperate for hope, inspiration and a desire to fulfill their purpose. This book will be God's timing for many who dare to open the pages and who dive into its truth.

This is more than another book to read and then put on a shelf. It's a manual for life and hope. It's an invitation for lasting change. Ready yourself for the journey and enjoy the ride and get ready to encounter God's grace for your life!

Sam Hinn

Pastor

INTRODUCTION

The song, *Amazing Grace*, has been and I am sure will be one of the greatest Christian hymns ever written. Written by a man so grateful and so amazed at the transforming power of God. It never ceases to bring tears and joy and gratitude. We all cry, "Thank you Lord for saving me." We are moved and moved again by the truth of it all.

But, amazing as it all is, there is more to grace than just saving grace, more to experience than just keeping grace! It is a wonderful provision by a loving God who clearly has opened a storehouse of his Goodness and mercy and sat his own son, our king, on its throne.

This book is actually written as a result of my encounters of the differing aspects of grace as the Holy Spirit, the Spirit of Grace himself, has revealed them to me. The scripture says it so beautifully:

> *" From the fullness of his grace, we have all received one blessing after another,"* John 1:16 NIV

When reading the original it actually says that we receive grace for grace. It actually means a grace that is replaced by a greater depth of grace again and again. From one realm to another!

I pray that my story will help others discover what an amazing, wonderful provision has been made for us.

CHAPTER 1

DISCOVERING THE GRACE OF GOD PERSONALLY

I have always been fascinated by the story of Moses having a face to face conversation with The Lord in Exodus 33. It has drawn me back to it again and again! Why? Because it shows us who our God really is and how a man can actually experience His glory in a personal way. Moses shows us how to push The Lord on his own promises. He cries out:

> *"...now show me your glory!"* Exodus 33:18

Compelling!! But it is the Lord's answer that we must discover. He answers Moses,

> *"I will cause all my goodness to pass by you, and proclaim my name, The Lord in your presence and I will be gracious to whom I will be gracious and I will show mercy to whom I will show mercy."* Exodus 33:19

There it is! That is who He is! He is so good that he cannot contain his grace. He has to show it, manifest it, and just plain share it.

The truth is that the song, *Amazing Grace*, is recorded by a man who was a slave trader and found the mercy of God and was saved in an extraordinary way. The grace of God and the mercy of God are inseparable! My story is, to me, as compelling as his. I was a violent drunkard, a drug user and pusher and all the things that go with that lifestyle. I stumbled into the message of the gospel and was brought into his mercy and grace. The preacher said to me, "Come chains and all!" Oh, like the hymn writer, Amazing Grace touched me, illuminated me and saved me.

Like so many, I lived for many years in the joy of this discovery. Especially knowing that there was a provision of a throne of grace and mercy where the King of Grace himself sat. Wow! How many times I came and asked for mercy and grace as The Lord was taking me from the old life of sin and all its dimensions. My pastor was right. I came chains and all. He broke the chains and went after the all!

That was only the beginning of my discovery which, in itself, was enough for a lifetime. As I have previously mentioned, there is more to grace than just the grace that saves and keeps. I was about to be brought into another personal revelation that, for me, opened a reservoir of life change and wonder when The Lord himself spoke to me and directed me into a personal breakthrough of immense proportions.

CHAPTER 2

THE GRACE TO SET ME FREE

I had visited the throne of grace time and time again but this had become more of a confessional. Mercy was rich. Mercy was received. As Hebrews 4:16 states, grace was to be found. Let me quote it:

> *"Therefore we come boldly to the throne of grace, where we receive mercy and find grace in a time of need."* Hebrews 4:16 (KJV).

The Lord was about to show me how to find the grace to stop the issue that needed mercy again and again.

Born in Ireland and of some definite Irish blood, I had inherited quite a temper. Then add some childhood issues and a life of violence and abuse. This had become a personal nightmare to me. Outside of Christ I had used the anger to control and cause fear but now that I had met The Lord it was a heart breaker. I tried to persuade myself that it was righteous anger I had but James 1 soon dismissed that!

"The anger of man does not fulfill the righteousness of God." James 1:21

Soon enough I realized I needed deliverance. Something was clearly beyond my control. I cannot even explain in this book what happened when ministered too…rage left me but the habit of anger was still with me.

I came to find myself weary of who I was, my wife severely wounded by my habits and my children scared. In desperation I walked out of my house one night and cried to my God to help me! As I walked down the hill outside my house I cried out, "Lord! Help me! Help me! How do I stop this?"

As I got to the bottom of the street I suddenly heard his voice clearly, "Grace!".

"Grace?", I said, thinking only of amazing grace but he repeated, "Grace."

So in obedience I cried out, "Give me grace, Lord give me grace."

Then he spoke again, " By faith we stand in this grace." Romans 5:2.

I said, "Really!?" I cried out again and in the dark, in the middle of the street, reached up my hands and by faith took the grace he was offering. No blinding light or power surge, just a strange feeling that something had happened. I walked up that hill a different man than I had gone down. I had been given a grace that broke the stronghold. Grace was discovered. A desperate man was given an awesome key.

After this I began to study grace afresh and loved the revelations that the scriptures had. Wow! In James 4:6 there is more grace! And again,

> **" From the fullness of his grace, we have all received one blessing after another,"** John 1:16 NIV

Scripture after scripture began to unlock. But another experience took me into another realm yet.

CHAPTER 3

THE REVELATION
THAT BLEW MY GRACE VIEW OFF ITS HINGES

I had now been serving The Lord for a good few years both in the UK and in the United States. I had traveled extensively but had become weary. Truthfully? I was weary of the wounds one collects in any form of ministry but particularly pastoral ministry. I had lost my joy, my hope and worst a sense of His presence. Added to that I was struggling greatly with my carnal nature, which often is the case when we struggle with wounds and hopelessness. I remember my wife saying that I looked miserable and that I needed to get myself fixed! Ouch...

During this time of my life I was visiting a friend in Little Rock Arkansas, Dr. Paul Doherty. A close friend indeed. I was also ministering in the church that he was pastoring. I went to bed in the hotel late and cried out one more time regarding my state. What am I to do? Help me Lord! Around 2 AM I awoke, which I had been doing for weeks normally to just lay awake for most of the night. But this night was different. The voice I had mentioned in the previous chapter, now spoke to me saying, "And great grace was on them all."

Knowing the voice and having had my previous experience, I instantly prayed, "Lord I receive that!", and went back to sleep. Wow, what another instant grace release! But more was yet to happen.

The next morning, I went for a walk to pray as I often do and of course I began to pray through what had happened the night before. I took the scripture from Hebrews,

> **'therefore let us come boldly to the throne of grace, to receive mercy and to find grace, in our hour of need'.**
> Hebrews 4:16

I prayed in faith over my issues and wounds. Suddenly a torrent of tears and freedom came. I wept for two hours and was able to forgive and release people and pain. Quite an experience, grace overflowed as I walked the streets weeping. The carnality was also touched, hopelessness released. But more, an overflowing grace began to flow out of me. Wherever I went and mentioned grace from that moment on, the Holy Spirit of grace Himself would move dramatically.

Yet there is more that came out of this encounter. First came the understanding of what Great Grace actually means. The word 'great' comes from the Greek word, 'megas', which means 'exceeding' or 'big' or 'overflowing'. The sense is that of being uncontainable. It comes from the passage in Acts 4, when the Holy Spirit so filled them that it went beyond them and the building shook. The next chapter Peter was so affected that his shadow brought healing to the sick. UNCONTAINED GRACE!!! That, to some measure, had happened to me and then flowed from me. More than that, I knew from my encounter and from the overflow of it that, once again, it was the intention of the Lord to flood the church with such a GREAT GRACE. "And Great Grace was on them all." That means one and all!

CHAPTER 4

MY GREATEST ENCOUNTER

When we first encounter Christ we clearly encounter the Spirit of Grace himself as he brings the Grace of Christ into our lives. Paul clearly states to the Romans that, without the Spirit of Christ, you do not belong to Him in Romans 8:9. Yet, there is more to encountering him than that! Clearly the encounter of Great Grace in Acts chapter 4 shows this.

I had, like so many saved in Pentecostal and Charismatic circles, been taught on the baptism of the Holy Spirit. I had experienced many in-fillings and touches of God but I wanted to know the Holy Spirit personally in a way I had not yet known. I had read of others such as Kathryn Kuhlman and Benny Hinn who spoke of their personal relationship with Him. As I read of these and heard testimonies I cried out and cried out. Many times He would touch me but I knew there was a greater relationship, so I sought Him for such an encounter. In fact, I had prayed not only to know Him but to so encounter Him in such a way that I could carry Him with me wherever I would travel and minister. Quite a prayer but, like Elisha, we should not limit our longings and desires!

On January 29th, 2008, I felt prompted one more time to go into the sanctuary to pray. (I remember the date well as it was the anniversary of my being a senior pastor years before.) One more time I said, "Oh Holy Spirit, I want to know You!" Suddenly a weight of presence sat on me, overwhelmed me and for hours, weeks and months filled me. He, the Holy Spirit of Grace, sat on me and the beginning of a new walk began with infilling after infilling, revelation upon revelation and relationship that was so personal and up close. He had heard my cry!

From that time I only had to mention what had happened and the atmosphere would be charged with His glorious presence. This was my encounter of all encounters. But more, when you encounter the Spirit of Grace so personally, He will unlock Grace to you in ways that are ever unfolding.

CHAPTER 5

MORE GRACE

As in any situation when the Lord begins to open a truth to you the door swings wide and revelation pours in. One such revelation is found in James,

> *" But he gives us more Grace."* James 4:6

The revelation, of course, is given regarding overcoming worldliness. But more Grace is the promise of John 1:16. Grace for grace.

Let's ponder a few scriptures:

REIGNING GRACE

"How much more they which receive abundance of Grace and of the gift of righteousness will reign in life by one, Jesus Christ." Romans 5:17

The context is,

" Where sin abounds, grace does much more about."

Romans 5:20

So there is a grace on offer for any and every realm!!

HE GIVES US MORE GRACE

Already quoted, but to overcome worldliness. Yes, there is a grace that enables you to stand against the spirit of the age!

ALL GRACE ABOUND

Wow, what a statement! All grace abound! The context? The ability to give beyond our ability. The grace to give that unlocks the grace of God to flow fully. The two chapters of 2 Corinthians 8 and 9, are a tremendous read on this revelation.

THE GRACE TO MINISTER

Paul speaks in Ephesians 3, of the grace that God gave him to minister. Again and again he explains what was given him. In verse 2, he speaks of the administration of God's grace given him.

So we see that there is Grace to overcome, Grace to unlock more Grace yet and Grace to minister. Yes, there is an unlimited Grace to walk in. So remember, there is always MORE GRACE!

CHAPTER 6

UNLOCKING THE TREASURE

What is the point of having a treasure chest if I cannot unlock it or a key to a lock box if there is not an address to where the box is kept? Such are the promises of Grace if there are no keys how to touch it.

There is a word that is used in the New Testament again and again that is paramount to touching our promises. I fell upon it while studying this great subject. It is the word 'Receive'.

> *"He came to his own and his own received him not. But to as many as received him, to them he gave the power to become the sons of God."* John 1:11-12

There it is! To receive or not to receive, that is the question!

The Greek word used for receive here is the word "Lambano". It means to see that which is offered and to take it and make it yours. We do it by faith. So many receive Christ by faith and then try to work for the rest of the promises when, truthfully, they all work in the same manner. See what is offered and in faith receive it! Romans 5:17, clearly states this. We reign in life when we receive the abundant provision of Grace! It worked for me when the Lord revealed his answer to my anger problem. It is the key! We ask for and receive what has been released by faith and there it is! Again and again and again. Whatever our circumstance. Whether fighting a sin or worldliness or taken beyond our own ability the throne is there and the promises are there but we must open our spirit to receive!

There are several other keys that are great helpers here, too. The Holy Spirit, who is the Spirit of Grace, will lead us into all the truth and helps us find the revelation of Grace needed at the time it is needed. We must ask Him! It should be our constant cry, " Spirit of truth lead me to the revelation of Grace."

The next key is this: We know the great promise that has been used so often,

> *"Faith comes by hearing and hearing by the word of God."* Romans 10:17

The specific word here for 'Word of God' is the word that means a specific word of God to you, or an utterance! "Rhēma": God speaking a word to you. We should always be asking what the actual word of the Lord is! It will bring Grace alongside its truth. In John 1:17, grace and truth came through Jesus. When a truth is revealed, it is coupled with grace to enable! Spirit of truth, Spirit of Grace, release to me a word of truth that will unlock the Grace needed.

CHAPTER 7

FINDING GRACE

I mentioned beforehand that I had found the throne of grace to be such a tremendous blessing. It is a place set by God where we could come and *receive* mercy not once but again and again. The word used for *receive*, is once again the Greek word "Lambano: To see what is on offer and take it for oneself". Mercy, according to Lamentations 3:23, is new every morning, which means it is limitless! We can come and receive again and again. Our subject is incredibly not just of mercy but of grace (which of course contains mercy). We receive mercy but 'find' grace. What we are being told is that we can always come for mercy but at the same throne there is a revelation of grace that when found is the answer to the constant need of mercy.

The word *'find'* used here in the Greek has multiple meanings. It is the Greek word *"Heuriskō: to find, get, obtain, perceive and see"*! It is a place where grace can be perceived and seen for oneself and then obtained and used to set one free and bring one into liberty in the matter that we seek mercy for. This actually is what happened to me both in my earlier encounter of being set free from the Irish temper and then again when I was touched by Great grace. But the truth is, that whatever brings us to this throne, there is at this place of God's provision a revelation of grace for any need! Awesome indeed.

Several very important aspects are involved in gaining these revelations. Firstly, we are told to approach the throne BOLDLY as sons. Not as paupers but as sons! This is our provision from our Heavenly Father. That means we should come expecting. Secondly, know that this is the place where the fullness of the grace of Jesus operates as mentioned in John 1:16. It is overflowing on our behalf. Thirdly, let's ask the Holy Spirit of Grace, the Revealer of Truth, to lead us into each revelation that we need. John 14:16 calls him the Helper, John 16:13 the Spirit of Truth and of course 1 Corinthians 2:9-12, says he is the revealer of the purposes of the Father. Yes, he is there to reveal each and every time we need another aspect of grace in our lives. Lastly and not least, know that this throne is operated by our High Priest who knows and sympathizes with our weaknesses, Hebrews 4:15.

I believe personally and emphatically that this grace is there to be, 'found'! Why should we have to search to find, you might ask? Surely it is already there for us. Because when we become involved in the search, we become owners of the revelation we find. It becomes ours! We possess it and it becomes part of our experience.

" Let us come boldly to the throne of grace, to receive mercy and find grace in a time of need."

CHAPTER 8

GRACE AND TRUTH

In John Chapter One, there is an incredible revelation of the way that grace can be appropriated. It is given as a revelation of the person of Jesus Christ himself. In verse 14 we are told that he is from the Father, filled with grace and truth. Then, in verse 17, we are told that the law came through Moses but grace and truth came through Jesus Christ. So much to grasp here but what I want to share is that grace and truth come together. This means that when the Lord reveals a truth grace comes with it, both to reveal it to you and also to enable you to grasp it and walk in it. Jesus brought the two together, but it has not been left there! He sent to us the Holy Spirit, the Spirit of grace and the Spirit of truth, so as the Holy Spirit reveals truth He enables by grace. Just talking about it makes me want to shout, "Hallelujah!". Grace and truth united and all for his people!

Let's look at how this becomes personal:

We are told in Romans 10:17, that faith comes by hearing and hearing by the Rhēma word of God. The word *Rhēma* there is "a specific utterance from God". Whether from the Logos word of God jumping out or the Holy Spirit speaking to you in any manner, it becomes an utterance to you. As this is released to you grace is released with it. Our job is to receive it by believing it and then grasp the grace that makes it a reality! So with every specific utterance to you grace comes to enable it to be your reality. When Romans Chapter 4 explains how Abraham was enabled to see the promise of God fulfilled we are told that,

> *"...against all hope in hope he believed..."*

> Romans 4:18

How could he do that? Because he was,

> *"...fully persuaded that God had power to do what He had promised."!* Romans 4:21

Awesome! He heard the utterance and then grace came and enabled him to believe but, more than that, enabled him to become what was spoken. God's ability released!

It is most interesting to study Hebrews chapter 12. It speaks of what we come to when we receive Christ and clearly states that we are receiving a kingdom that cannot be shaken in verse 28. There is that Greek word, *Lambanō,* again but this time using *paralambanō: something that draws near that we receive.*

How? Ready for it?

"... see to it that you do not refuse him who speaks." Hebrews 12:25

When He speaks, His Kingdom operates around His spoken truth. The Word goes on to say,

> **"...let us have grace..."** Hebrews 12:28

There they are again, grace and truth together. He speaks. It releases an area of his kingdom and grace is there to enable us to believe and receive.

When this amazing truth is grasped, we realize that the promise of John chapter 1 verse 16, becomes non-stop operative. Grace to grace!

CHAPTER 9

THE GRACE OF GIVING

I have now, by God's grace, been in the ministry over 40 years and have heard so many people talk about the grace of giving. Some speak of it because they have found its immense truth. Others talk of it because they try to use grace as a reason to actually not give. I talk here of my journey into this immense truth.

I had actually been born again just a few months and had started attending the Sunday morning meeting in our local church. Up until this time I had only been Sunday nights which was, in those days, a "gospel only" meeting. It was much like the seeker friendly services of today. Any mention of money was to just take an offering during announcement time. You basically threw in what loose change you had. But the Sunday morning meeting was the believers' meeting! This was a heavier, worship-based service with deeper preaching of the word and then there was teaching on giving. Here it came! That word, "tithing"! "Tithing!", I said to myself. "That is nothing more than Old Testament law!" But me being me, I took it to the Lord seeking to persuade him of my view.

I was weeding the garden of my mother in law at the time and letting God know what I thought about it all when, to my shock, he spoke directly back to me. "What about Abraham?" Wow, was not expecting that! Abraham was before the law and he tithed to Melchizedek. So, as mentioned in the last chapter on grace and truth, the truth hit me and the grace enabled me to start a life of giving.

Tithing and offerings became such a part of my life. Indeed, the fruit was almost instant as I saw the hand of God meet me again and again. I could actually write a whole book on the provision of God. The years of proof! Yet, the truth of the grace of giving became a reality to me, too. Who could not read about the Macedonian churches in 2 Corinthians chapter 8 and not be fascinated? They were enabled by grace to give beyond their means. They precipitated the revelation written in 2 Corinthians 9:8, the promise of all grace being released. What on earth is this? Well, we must remember that grace is the enablement by God to do what we can't do. We become affected by his heart to give.

"...for God so loved he gave..." John 3:16

Then a faith touches us to go beyond the normal and see the hand of God provide. The first few verses of 2 Corinthians chapter 8 actually shows us how this operates. 2 Corinthians 8:5, shows us that these people were first given to God and then to the work and people of God. Paul was really touched by them. It was stirred by their desire to minister to others we are told in verse 3. As a result, we are told in verse 2 it welled up into immense liberality within their means and beyond. Paul says in verse 1 that this is a grace given by God.

The grace of giving is grace in action! It so loves God, his work and his people that it constantly wants to be a blessing whenever and wherever it can. It operates often beyond reason and has a faith that God will supply for more. This verse sums up this faith:

> *"He who supplies seed to the sower and bread for food, will supply and multiply your seed for sowing. You will be enriched in every way to be generous in every way."* 2 Corinthians 9: 10 and 11 ESV.

This is a grace that open doors of blessing to you and others and causes a constant flow of the goodness of God.

CHAPTER 10

I AM WHAT I AM BY THE GRACE OF GOD

Wow was I in for a shock! The ministry, the call of God, came upon me early after my salvation but I was not ready to be compared with other ministries and evaluated by expectations. I remember so well my early years of pastoring. I began to fear the phone calls by one of the older deacons telling me how I had missed it or... But the experience that really brought it to a head was when a couple of congregation members of the new church I was pastoring came to me to ask me why I was not more like the pastor that had left. They explained to me the differences. But that was just it! We **were** different... different gifts from God, different personalities. Each of us had a different grace. Several years later, the Lord himself brought the truth home to me in a personal way. I was about to walk away from the ministry for good. I had become a performer rather than a gift given by God. I was trying to be what everyone said a minister was supposed to be. I found that Americans had even stronger views than the British. Then the Lord shared this beautiful

scripture with me,

> *"But by the grace of God, I am what I am..."*
>
> 1 Corinthians 15:10

Bam! I am and can only be what I am graced to be! A

pastor cannot be a prophet. He can prophesy but he is not

graced to be a prophet. We can only walk in our grace and

not someone else's. Suddenly after years of anguish, I was

free to be me. Me and nobody else.

Grace shapes us and grace teaches us and grace enables

us. We are not a copy, not a shadow. We are uniquely us.

When we become what grace enables us to become, we

then can walk in peace and integrity. Paul carries on to

say,

> *",,,and his grace towards me was not in vain."*
>
> 1 Corinthians 15:10

Once Paul caught it, he walked it and relied on it and

ministered from it. I cannot be what God has graced

others to be. I am only responsible for the grace I have

been bestowed. It does not matter if even I have a

preference. I am only what I am, not my preference, not your preference. I am a result of the grace given me. I must walk it and live in it.

Performance and competition have unfortunately become part of the way of life here in the west. Big is better. We often even equate success with size rather than obedience. The result: we stop being ourselves and try to emulate the one who seems to be successful. But what if we don't have their grace? We cannot keep the act up for long before we crash like a plane with engine malfunction. No, friends, we rob ourselves by doing such things but more rob the church and world of our true grace. Grace is multicolored we are told in 1 Peter 4:10. Our color is unique, beautiful and belongs to us and we are the only ones who can function in it.

Surely it is time to overflow in our grace, for there we will find grace. Copies be gone! Originals arise! Church and people be now blessed by our absolute uniqueness!

CHAPTER 11

MY GRACE IS SUFFICIENT FOR YOU

Any student of the word has no doubt visited one of the

most significant statements given concerning grace in the

Bible and particularly the New Testament when Paul,

under great duress, cries out aloud. In fact, he does so

three separate times. The scripture says he had been

buffeted by a message of satan.

> *"And lest I should be exalted above measure*
>
> *through the abundance of the revelations, there*
>
> *was given to me a thorn in the flesh, the*
>
> *messenger of Satan to buffet me, lest I should be*
>
> *exalted above measure".* 2 Corinthians 12:7 kjv

The word *buffet* there is *like a person being punched and*

punched. All a boxer can do is place himself in a position

of defense. His cry for help brought an amazing revelation

from the Lord.

"My grace is sufficient for you, my strength is made perfect in weakness." 2 Corinthians 12:9

Grace, it is revealed, has a sufficiency for any circumstance and situation when tapped into.

The truth alone is awesome but when grace becomes personal it adds another dimension. This is how this scripture and revelation became so personal to me. I was traveling to minister in Connecticut for several days when suddenly, out of the blue...out of nowhere, I became ill while on the plane. I was so sick that I had to stop traveling and stay in Chicago airport where I slept a total of 18 hours trying to recuperate. The following day I had to start ministering but I was so weak. This sickness had come on the back of years of ministry with very little break and I was worn out. All I could say was thank God for the anointing. But I was so weak! But as the days went on it was too much. I lay down and cried out to God in my weakness. I knew without help that I wouldn't be able to do all that was asked of me. I suddenly heard this song that had been given to my daughter by an Angel when she was broken and desperate. The song was simple. "In times of weakness, in times of storm, just lift your hands and praise the Lord." I sang it and sang it. I began to feel strength come into me. Then the Lord reminded me of that scripture. I began to pray it over and over. Suddenly his grace not only met me but the strength of the Lord came through me. Oh boy did it go through me! The word *strength* is actually the Greek word , *dunamis* , from which we get the word *power*. The results were staggering in the next meeting. The tangible presence of God began to manifest.

Jesus so clearly stated that knowing truth comes by walking truth.

> **"To the Jews who had believed him, Jesus said,**
> **'If you hold to my teaching, you are really my**

*disciples. **Then you will know the truth, and the truth will set you free'.*** John 8:31,32

This, like so many truths, came by revelation and experience. When in any situation we rely on his grace and not ourselves and when we reach in faith to grasp it then grace is there to be experienced. Weakness, which we so despise, is the key to the Spirit of Grace manifesting himself and empowering us beyond ourselves. But it takes the embracing of weakness to unlock such manifestations. Paul says in this same passage that he had learned to do such a thing and the results were eternal.

So, if his grace is sufficient may we come to the table of his grace whether walking a valley or a mountain top or whatever? With grace comes all the power and life of God. Lord, we rely on your sufficiency. We reach out in our weakness. Look out! The hand of God is beginning to move....

CHAPTER 12

GROWING IN GRACE

There is nothing like waking up early in the morning with scriptures on your mind. Of course, I know it happens to us all. But this morning was different. It wouldn't leave me alone. Here is the scripture:

> *"But grow in the grace and the knowledge of the Lord Jesus Christ. To him be glory both now and forever."* 2 Peter 3:18

It is saying as we grow in his grace we bring more glory to him!

Growth in anything covers two things. One is by revelation and the second by experience. For us to grow in grace we need more revelation of grace. The Spirit of grace and the word of God revealing all that there is for us. The scripture we just read ties this revelation alongside a growth of our knowledge of the one who manifested grace himself, Jesus Christ. The more we know him, the more his grace will be revealed. Equally, the more we walk with the Spirit of grace who is the Holy Spirit, the more manifestation we will encounter. Fellowship with the Holy Spirit will bring untold revelation and manifestation.

> "May the grace of the lord Jesus Christ, and the love of God, and the fellowship of the Holy Spirit be with you all." 2 Corinthians 13:14

Perhaps one of the most fascinating scriptures of growth in grace is found in John. I will use the King James Version for a moment here.

> "And of his fullness we have all we received grace for grace." John 1:16 KJV

Simple translation: His grace knew no bounds and is uncontainable. It overflows. It manifests to us by ever increasing grace or grace that replaces a former level of grace dependant on our walk and on our need. But once again this grace must be received! Once again it is the Greek word *Lambano*. See the grace offered and then *reach in and receive*. Literally there is no end to the growth that we can have because there is no end to the overflow of his grace! Awesome....

If we want more, there is more! If we desire it, if we need it then we can have it. Going back to our scripture, it is actually a command: "But grow in the grace!" There it is! The more we grow, the more he is glorified. So, to not grow brings him less glory but the more grace there is the more he is seen in us. Not a choice. A demand! Let's join in with what Peter is telling us. Let us, like Peter, desire to grow!!

More grace is the promise of James 1:6, and more grace is the overflow from the throne of grace in John 1:16, so more grace is what we desire and need and want and pray for.

CHAPTER 13

GRACE FOR THE RACE

This came into my heart so strongly one Sunday morning:

"Grace for the race!" A scripture quickly sprung to mind. It

was the famous Hebrews 11 and 12 combination.

Hebrews 11 being, of course, the renowned chapter of

the heroes of faith but then bridging into Hebrews 12 and

the race set before us. We are told these guys not only

ran their race but are a cloud of witnesses watching ours.

The race set before us…

> *"Therefore, since we are surrounded by such a*
>
> *great cloud of witnesses, let us throw off*
>
> *everything that hinders and the sin that so easily*
>
> *entangles. And let us run with perseverance the*
>
> *race marked out for us…"* Hebrews 12:1

The Greek word, *race*, used here is actually used 5 times

in the New Testament. In four of the times used it is

translated as *fight or conflict* but this time it is translated *race* due to this context where we are told to run it. The basis was that of the games from which we get the Olympics. So, our race is not just a plain run but that of overcoming and fighting through. In fact, the whole chapter highlights some of the things we have to overcome, from hindrances and sin to hardships and weariness. We are warned of opposition and rough paths. Quite a race! But it is our race, given us, not belonging to somebody else. Our race is what is before us and it is ours to run. When we read of all the issues in this race we wonder why it was not called a battle. It is clearly a race and has a goal. What is that goal? To finish and fulfill our calling. We are told it will take two things: One will be perseverance (in verse 1) and the other grace (in verse 15)!

> *"See to it that no one falls short of the grace of God and that no bitter root grows up to cause trouble and defile many."* Hebrews 12:15

Grace? Yes, grace for the race! We are told in this verse

not to miss the grace of God, which means we can get so

caught up in the race and hardships and trials that we

miss the very grace released to us to finish and overcome.

To each of us God releases a grace for our race! How can

we make sure we don't miss it? We are told in verse 2 to

"Look at the author and finisher of our faith" (race), Jesus

himself. He who brought "grace and truth" and whom

from his throne exudes overflowing grace.

> *"Out of his fullness we have all received grace in*
>
> *place of grace already given. For the law was*
>
> *given through Moses; grace and truth came*
>
> *through Jesus Christ."* John 1: 16-17.

He, this same Jesus, is the author and finisher or our race.

He it is, who releases a grace for our race! As we look to

him he will reveal the grace needed and bless us with it

on our journey. It is his throne of grace found in Hebrews.

> *"Let us then approach God's throne of grace with*
>
> *confidence, so that we may receive mercy and find*

grace to help us in our time of need." Hebrews

4:16

As we run our race and encounter various obstacles we

seek to *find* the grace needed at his throne. Awesome!

And, as previously mentioned, all that while receiving

mercy! Yes! There is a grace for our race. Let's not miss it!

It is prepared for us and ready to be obtained on the

journey!

CONCLUSION

When we are launched by the Lord into the amazing journey of grace, we enter a realm that is ever growing and fresh revelations await us. Peter tells us,

> *"...grow in the grace and knowledge of our Lord and Savior Jesus Christ."* 2 Peter 3:18.

Grace starts with him and finishes with him! But we can grow it as we grow in our knowledge of him.

Let's always remember, too, that from his throne grace ever flows,

> *"For from his fullness we have all received, grace upon grace."* John 1:16.

There is an endless flowing supply. We grow in it as we need it. We also grow in it as we use it. 1 Peter 4:10 shows us to use our grace so that it can be manifested in all its beauty. It was the use of grace from the Macedonians that opened the heavens. The simple sowing and reaping principle is always at work.

I really like the King James version:

"…from grace to grace." John 1:16

Growing and abounding and then growing and abounding more in grace. The grace you see in me today should be miniature compared to what should be seen as I mature in my God. We are all living epistles of grace and the letter is continually to be written.

Yes, indeed grace becomes very personal!

BIOGRAPHY

Dennis Paul Goldsworthy-Davis has been blessed to travel extensively throughout the world ministering both apostolically and prophetically to the body of Christ. He operates within a strong governmental prophetic office and frequently sees the Presence of God and the Spirit of Revival break out upon the lives of people. Dennis has equally been graced to relate to many spiritual sons throughout the earth, bringing wisdom, guidance and encouragement.

Born in Southern Ireland and raised in England, Dennis was radically saved from a life of drugs and violence in 1973. Soon after his conversion, he began to operate within his local church where he was fathered spiritually by Bennie Finch, a seasoned apostolic minister. After working in youth ministry Dennis pastored in several areas within the U.K. It was during these pastorates that Dennis began to see profound moves of God in these same venues.

In 1986 Dennis experienced a dramatic shift in his life and ministry. He and his family moved to San Antonio, Texas, to join a vibrant, functioning apostolic team. In 1990 Dennis was commissioned to start Great Grace International Christian Center, a local work in San Antonio. Dennis continues to serve as the Senior /Minister of GGICC and heads the formation of the apostolic team in the local house. Presently, Dennis relates to several functioning apostolic ministries. He draws wisdom and accountability from Robert Henderson of Global Reformers, Barry Wissler of HarvestNet International and for many years Alan Vincent. Each of these carry strong, well-seasoned apostolic offices in their own right.

Dennis has been married to his wife Christine since 1973 and has two wonderful daughters and three grandchildren.

Made in the USA
Monee, IL
22 February 2022

91584109R00039